# CONTENTS

## OVERVIEW

*What's Your Point of View?* is a four-book series built around themes that all students will enjoy learning and thinking about. The titles are:

- *What's Your Point of View on School Issues?*
- *What's Your Point of View on Community Issues?*
- *What's Your Point of View on the Environment?*
- *What's Your Point of View on Careers?*

Each book presents three issues that center around real-life stories and current information. Students read about the issue and learn how to use the critical thinking process. They make their own decisions and form their own points of view. Through a variety of interesting activities, all designed to build critical thinking skills, students sharpen their abilities to put information to use.

Students are encouraged to:
- read for meaning
- learn new words
- collect facts
- organize information
- analyze
- apply knowledge
- summarize
- evaluate
- communicate ideas

### What are the objectives of this series?
- to present information in a variety of ways
- to help students learn how to find the information they need to make logical decisions
- to teach students how to use information and the critical thinking process effectively
- to build the understanding that problems related to issues often do not have one simple solution
- to encourage students to communicate their ideas
- to show students that people may have different points of view about issues

### What are the issues?
School issues:
- *What a Sport!*
  Focuses on equal rights for boys and girls.
- *Don't Flunk Lunch!*
  Focuses on making school lunch menus healthier.

- *A Longer School Year?*
  Focuses on lengthening the school year.

*Community issues:*
- *Does Every Vote Count?*
  Focuses on voting and reasons why many Americans do not vote.
- *Buckle Up for Safety!*
  Focuses on the use of seat belts and the law.
- *The American Way*
  Focuses on civic-mindedness and getting involved with the community.

*Environment issues:*
- *The Cleanup Kids!*
  Focuses on recycling and getting involved to protect the environment.
- *What's in the Water?*
  Focuses on protecting our water from pollution.
- *It's a Crime!*
  Focuses on protecting the environment in the workplace.

*Career issues:*
- *Go For It!*
  Focuses on success, overcoming obstacles, self-esteem, and maintaining a positive attitude.
- *Looking Ahead*
  Focuses on the how the workplace is changing because of new inventions and technology.
- *More Jobs or Good Jobs?*
  Focuses on preparing students for jobs in the workplace.

### How are the issues organized?
Throughout each book, information for each issue is carefully presented in a logical order to build critical thinking skills. Each issue presents:

- *Words to Know*—Vocabulary words are presented with concise definitions. Each word defined in this section appears in boldface the first time it appears in the selection.
- *The selection*—Students read about the issue and use the selection as a basis for the lesson.
- *Checking Your Understanding* (Comprehension)—Multiple-choice questions check understanding and recall.
- *Choosing an Issue*—Three issues give students the opportunity to choose one issue to focus on throughout the lesson.
- *Getting the Facts* (Collecting information)—Students learn how to look, listen, recall the story, and ask questions.

- *Organizing the Information* (Organization)—The use of charts, sequencing, and comparing and contrasting are some of the skills students learn and apply in this section.
- *Taking a Closer Look* (Analysis)—Students build skills by identifying facts and opinions, finding cause and effect, and identifying the pros and cons. The pros and cons in this section are especially helpful to students for forming their own point of view.
- *Thinking Other Ways* (Application)—By thinking about situations in different ways, students learn how to reason and solve problems.
- *Telling It Your Way* (Synthesis)—Students summarize important information and relate it to what they already know.
- *Deciding What Is Important* (Evaluation)—By reviewing the information from the previous sections, looking at the pros and cons, and answering questions that they support with facts or details, students begin the evaluation process.
- *What's Your Point of View?*—Based on all the information they learned and decisions they made throughout the activities, students write their own point of view and share their ideas with the class.

*Checkpoints* guide and help students understand the steps of the information gathering process as they proceed through the analysis of the issue. Encourage students to follow each checkpoint.

Students are also encouraged to brainstorm as they *Think about this…*and *Talk about…*other topics that relate to their own lives.

*Going a little further…*at the end of each issue contains additional motivating activities for students to do on their own, with a partner, in groups, or with the entire class.

*Putting It Together…*appears at the end of each book. Refer the students to this summary of the critical-thinking process. They can use the process to shape their viewpoints about other academic issues or those issues which immediately affect their lives.

## What is critical thinking?

Critical thinking is a step-by-step process that all students can learn and use to put information together in a way that is meaningful and relevant to their lives. *What's Your Point of View?* builds a foundation for critical thinking. Students become informed about issues they face today, and learn how to deal with the issues they may face tomorrow.

Through this critical thinking process, students *collect, organize, analyze, apply, synthesize,* and *evaluate* the information presented. By sharpening their critical thinking skills, all students learn how to solve problems, make decisions, and communicate effectively.

## How will you meet the needs of all students?

Ideally, working through all of the pages in the lesson is preferred. However, these steps do not have to be followed in order. Since critical thinking skills are not necessarily categorized in order of importance, one skill may be used in place of another. In other instances, only a few skills may be needed for critical thinking or for solving a problem. The issues in this book take a step-by-step approach. Be sure that students understand the entire process before using the steps out of sequence or before skipping any of the skills.

Some students may find the critical thinking process easier than others, once they have worked through at least one of the issues. The *Skills Mastery Chart* on pages 7 and 8 will show you what pages students need to complete in each section before they can move on to the next section successfully. For example, students may only need to complete through page 3 before they move on to pages 4–7, or they may need to complete through page 7 before they move on to pages 10–12. You can use all or any part of the *Going a Little Further…* section at any time.

This chart is also useful for helping students who may be having difficulty understanding a specific part of the process. Review only those sections that are trouble spots to ensure learning.

## How can the issues be used to build skills?

The *Scope and Sequence of Critical-Thinking Skills* on page 6 will help you find the pages that teach a specific skill. Use this chart to help you with your lesson plans.

## SCOPE AND SEQUENCE OF CRITICAL THINKING SKILLS

| | SCHOOL | COMMUNITY | ENVIRONMENT | CAREER |
|---|---|---|---|---|
| **COLLECTING INFORMATION** | | | | |
| Focusing on the Topic | 3; 4B; 17; 21; 22B; 37; 42 43B; 57 | 3; 4B; 17; 21; 22B; 37; 41; 42B; 57 | 3; 4B; 17; 21; 22B; 37; 41 42B; 57 | 3; 4B; 19; 23; 24B; 39; 43 44B; 57 |
| Recalling | 4T; 6; 22T; 24; 43T; 45; 46T | 4T; 6; 22T; 24T; 25; 42T 44; 48 | 4T; 6B; 22T 23; 24B; 28; 42T; 44, 45T; 48 | 4T; 6; 24T 26B; 46 |
| Observing | 5T; 23; 33; 44; 50 | 5T; 23; 43 | 5; 9; 23; 43; 59#4 | 5; 25; 45 |
| Questioning | 7; 25; 46B | 7; 26; 45 | 7; 25; 45B | 7–8; 27; 47 |
| Listening | 5B; 24T; 45M | 5B; 24B; 43B; | 6T; 24T; 44T | 5B; 25B; 46T |
| Researching | 19#2; 39#2; 46B–47; 59#1–2 | 19#2; 27; 39#2 | 19#1; 23; 24T; 39; 59#2–3 | 21#3; 41#2–3 59#1 |
| **ORGANIZING INFORMATION** | | | | |
| Representing Information | 8; 39#1–3; 50 | 8–9; 28 | 8; 26–27; 29B; 47B | 28 |
| Organizing Details | 27 | 32; 46; 50 | 8; 26–27; 31 | 9, 48 |
| Using Compare and Contrast | 48–49 | 8–9; 29 | 28; 31 | 29–30 |
| Categorizing | 28; 39#1 | 47; 59#2 | 47; 59#1–2 | 10 |
| Sequencing | 9 | 47 | 8; 15T; 47 | 9; 49 |
| **ANALYZING INFORMATION** | | | | |
| Identifying Key Points | 12B | 30B | 12B; 25; 29B; 47B; 48 | 11, 48 |
| Determining Fact and Opinion | 10; 30; 51 | 10; 30T; 48 | 10; 29T; 48 | 11; 31; 50 |
| Finding Supporting Details | 17; 27; 37; 57 | 17; 32; 37; 46; 57 | 17; 32; 37; 46; 57 | 19; 39; 48; 57 |
| Identifying Main Ideas | 32 | 46 | 25 | 48 |
| Recognizing Pros and Cons | 16; 19#4; 36; 52B | 11; 16; 31; 36; 49; 56 | 11; 16; 30; 36; 49–50; 56 | 12; 18; 32–33; 38; 56 |
| Identifying Cause and Effect | 12T; 31 | 12; 51 | 12T; 51 | 13B; 34; 52 |
| Analyzing Different Points of View | 19#3–4; 52T | 39#3 | 31 | 21#4; 41#1 |
| **APPLYING INFORMATION** | | | | |
| Predicting | 13, 33; 53 | 13; 33; 52 | 13; 32; 34T; 52 | 14–15; 35; 53 |
| Reasoning | 13, 29; 33; 44; 53; 55B; 59#1–3 | 13; 33; 52 | 13; 32; 52 | 14–15; 35; 53 |
| Inferring | 33; 35B | 32; 50; 52 | 14T | 11B |
| Problem Solving | 19#4; 33 | 19#3; 39#1; 59#2 | 33; 52 | 16; 21#1–2; 21#4; 59 |
| Restructuring | 13; 33; 35T; 53 | 13; 33; 35; 52–54 | 13; 32–33; 52–54 | 14–15; 35–36; 53–54 |
| Relating to Real-Life Situations | 14B; 15B; 19 35; 39; 53; 59 | 8–9; 15B; 19; 39; 59 | 9; 14B; 15; 19; 31–34; 35B; 39; 52–54; 59 | 15–16; 17B; 21; 36B; 41; 45; 54; 55B; 59 |
| **SYNTHESIZING INFORMATION** | | | | |
| Summarizing Important Elements | 15T; 17; 35T; 37; 55; 57 | 15T, 17; 35T; 37; 55; 57 | 15T; 17; 35T; 37; 55; 57 | 17T;19; 37T; 39; 55T; 57 |
| Integrating Information | 15; 35; 55 | 15; 35; 55 | 15; 35; 55 | 17; 37; 55 |
| **EVALUATING INFORMATION** | | | | |
| Establishing Criteria | 16; 36; 56 | 16, 36; 56; 59#1 | 16; 36; 56 | 18; 38; 56 |
| Making Judgements | 17; 19#1; 37; 57 | 17, 19#1; 37; 57 | 17; 37; 39#3; 57 | 19; 39; 57 |
| Forming an Opinion | 18, 38, 58 | 18; 38; 58 | 18; 38; 58 | 20; 40; 58 |
| Evaluating the Outcome | 18; 26; 38; 58 | 18; 38; 58 | 18; 38; 58 | 20; 40; 58 |
| Communicating | 14B; 15; 18; 19; 34B; 35; 38; 39; 47; 54B; 55; 58; 59 | 14B; 15; 18; 19 34B; 35; 38; 39 54B; 55; 58; 59 | 14B; 15; 18; 19; 34B; 35; 38; 39; 54B; 55; 58; 59 | 16B; 17; 20; 21; 36B; 37; 40; 41; 54B; 55, 58; 59 |

(T=TOP; B=BOTTOM; M=MIDDLE)

# SKILLS MASTERY CHART

Students should complete activities up to the page indicated next to each skill before proceeding to the next section.

## SCHOOL

| ISSUE 1 ACTIVITY PAGES | 4–7 | 8–9 | 10–12 | 13–14 | 15 | 16–17 | 18 | 19 |
|---|---|---|---|---|---|---|---|---|
| COLLECTING | 3 | | | | | | | |
| ORGANIZING | | 3 | | | | | | |
| ANALYZING | | | 7 | | | | | |
| APPLYING | | | | 3 | | | | |
| SYNTHESIZING | | | | | 3 | | | |
| EVALUATING | | | | | | 12 | 17 | |
| EXTENDING | | | | | | | | 3 |

| ISSUE 2 ACTIVITY PAGES | 22–26 | 27–29 | 30–32 | 33–34 | 35 | 36–37 | 38 | 39 |
|---|---|---|---|---|---|---|---|---|
| COLLECTING | 21 | | | | | | | |
| ORGANIZING | | 21 | | | | | | |
| ANALYZING | | | 26 | | | | | |
| APPLYING | | | | 21 | | | | |
| SYNTHESIZING | | | | | 21 | | | |
| EVALUATING | | | | | | 32 | 37 | |
| EXTENDING | | | | | | | | 21 |

| ISSUE 3 ACTIVITY PAGES | 43–47 | 48–50 | 51–52 | 53–54 | 55 | 56–57 | 58 | 59 |
|---|---|---|---|---|---|---|---|---|
| COLLECTING | 42 | | | | | | | |
| ORGANIZING | | 42 | | | | | | |
| ANALYZING | | | 47 | | | | | |
| APPLYING | | | | 42 | | | | |
| SYNTHESIZING | | | | | 42 | | | |
| EVALUATING | | | | | | 52 | 57 | |
| EXTENDING | | | | | | | | 42 |

## COMMUNITY

| ISSUE 1 ACTIVITY PAGES | 4–7 | 8–9 | 10–12 | 13–14 | 15 | 16–17 | 18 | 19 |
|---|---|---|---|---|---|---|---|---|
| COLLECTING | 3 | | | | | | | |
| ORGANIZING | | 3 | | | | | | |
| ANALYZING | | | 7 | | | | | |
| APPLYING | | | | 3 | | | | |
| SYNTHESIZING | | | | | 3 | | | |
| EVALUATING | | | | | | 12 | 17 | |
| EXTENDING | | | | | | | | 3 |

| ISSUE 2 ACTIVITY PAGES | 22–27 | 28–29 | 30–32 | 33–34 | 35 | 36–37 | 38 | 39 |
|---|---|---|---|---|---|---|---|---|
| COLLECTING | 21 | | | | | | | |
| ORGANIZING | | 21 | | | | | | |
| ANALYZING | | | 27 | | | | | |
| APPLYING | | | | 21 | | | | |
| SYNTHESIZING | | | | | 21 | | | |
| EVALUATING | | | | | | 32 | 37 | |
| EXTENDING | | | | | | | | 21 |

| ISSUE 3 ACTIVITY PAGE | 42–45 | 46–47 | 48–51 | 52–54 | 55 | 56–57 | 58 | 59 |
|---|---|---|---|---|---|---|---|---|
| COLLECTING | 41 | | | | | | | |
| ORGANIZING | | 41 | | | | | | |
| ANALYZING | | | 45 | | | | | |
| APPLYING | | | | 41 | | | | |
| SYNTHESIZING | | | | | 41 | | | |
| EVALUATING | | | | | | 51 | 57 | |
| EXTENDING | | | | | | | | 41 |

## SKILLS MASTERY CHART

Students should complete activities up to the page indicated next to each skill before proceeding to the next section.

### ENVIRONMENT

| ISSUE 1 ACTIVITY PAGES | 4–7 | 8–9 | 10–12 | 13–14 | 15 | 16–17 | 18 | 19 |
|---|---|---|---|---|---|---|---|---|
| COLLECTING | 3 | | | | | | | |
| ORGANIZING | | 3 | | | | | | |
| ANALYZING | | | 7 | | | | | |
| APPLYING | | | | 3 | | | | |
| SYNTHESIZING | | | | | 3 | | | |
| EVALUATING | | | | | | 12 | 17 | |
| EXTENDING | | | | | | | | 3 |

| ISSUE 2 ACTIVITY PAGES | 22–25 | 26–28 | 29–31 | 32–34 | 35 | 36–37 | 38 | 39 |
|---|---|---|---|---|---|---|---|---|
| COLLECTING | 21 | | | | | | | |
| ORGANIZING | | 21 | | | | | | |
| ANALYZING | | | 25 | | | | | |
| APPLYING | | | | 21 | | | | |
| SYNTHESIZING | | | | | 21 | | | |
| EVALUATING | | | | | | 31 | 37 | |
| EXTENDING | | | | | | | | 21 |

| ISSUE 3 ACTIVITY PAGES | 42–45 | 46–47 | 48–51 | 52–54 | 55 | 56–57 | 58 | 59 |
|---|---|---|---|---|---|---|---|---|
| COLLECTING | 41 | | | | | | | |
| ORGANIZING | | 41 | | | | | | |
| ANALYZING | | | 41 | | | | | |
| APPLYING | | | | 41 | | | | |
| SYNTHESIZING | | | | | 41 | | | |
| EVALUATING | | | | | | 51 | 57 | |
| EXTENDING | | | | | | | | 41 |

### CAREER

| ISSUE 1 ACTIVITY PAGES | 4–8 | 9–10 | 11–13 | 14–16 | 17 | 18–19 | 20 | 121 |
|---|---|---|---|---|---|---|---|---|
| COLLECTING | 3 | | | | | | | |
| ORGANIZING | | 3 | | | | | | |
| ANALYZING | | | 8 | | | | | |
| APPLYING | | | | 3 | | | | |
| SYNTHESIZING | | | | | 3 | | | |
| EVALUATING | | | | | | 13 | 19 | |
| EXTENDING | | | | | | | | 3 |

| ISSUE 2 ACTIVITY PAGES | 24–27 | 28–30 | 31–34 | 35–36 | 37 | 38–39 | 40 | 341 |
|---|---|---|---|---|---|---|---|---|
| COLLECTING | 23 | | | | | | | |
| ORGANIZING | | 23 | | | | | | |
| ANALYZING | | | 27 | | | | | |
| APPLYING | | | | 23 | | | | |
| SYNTHESIZING | | | | | 23 | | | |
| EVALUATING | | | | | | 34 | 39 | |
| EXTENDING | | | | | | | | 23 |

| ISSUE 3 ACTIVITY PAGES | 44–47 | 48–49 | 50–52 | 53–54 | 55 | 56–57 | 58 | 59 |
|---|---|---|---|---|---|---|---|---|
| COLLECTING | 43 | | | | | | | |
| ORGANIZING | | 43 | | | | | | |
| ANALYZING | | | 47 | | | | | |
| APPLYING | | | | 43 | | | | |
| SYNTHESIZING | | | | | 43 | | | |
| EVALUATING | | | | | | 52 | 57 | |
| EXTENDING | | | | | | | | 43 |

# WHAT'S YOUR POINT OF VIEW ON SCHOOL ISSUES?

## ISSUE 1    What a Good Sport!

*Summary:* This story discusses whether it is appropriate for a boy to play on an all-girl sports team. In this case, George, a high-school student, was unable to join the football team, and decided to join the girl's field hockey team. He had previous experience with street hockey, and was a good player. School district lawyers decided George could play on the team, but he had to follow field hockey uniform requirements: he had to wear a skirt. The story discusses the various opinions of the coaches, teammates, and the public in general.

*Background Information:* This story focuses on equality of the sexes. The focus happens to be a boy on a girls' team, but the reverse is also commonplace. Since the 1970s, organized clubs and sports institutions have been forced to open their membership up to both sexes. In some cases, this has been voluntary, but in others, courts have had to decide. Topics for further class discussion can include:

- Women's suffrage movement of the early 20th century
- Equal Rights Amendment movement of the 1960's-1970's
- Father's Rights (as stay-at-home parents, after childbirth, etc.)
- N.O.W. (National Organization of Women)
- Boy Scouts of America/ Girl Scouts of America membership
- Co-ed professional sports teams

## ENRICHMENT ACTIVITY

Stage a mock trial in the classroom. The trial will determine whether Jane Doe, a girl, will be allowed to join the Camp-About Boys' Club, an all-boys social club. You, the teacher, will be the judge. Select one female student to play the role of Jane Doe, and one male student to play the role of Joe Smith, leader of the local Camp-About Club. Have the class select one male student as the lawyer for the boys' side, and one female student as the lawyer for the girls' side. The remainder of the class will serve as witnesses.

Arrange the classroom so that you are placed at the front of the class, by the board. A chair for testimony of witnesses should be placed beside you. The lawyers should face the class as they speak. Allow the lawyers a few minutes to select one or two students to play witnesses for their side. Then have the girls' side begin questioning witnesses and presenting their case, followed by the boys' side. While the lawyers and witnesses are discussing the case, listen and write the statements that you feel are pro or con on the board. At the end of the trial, you decide the case based on the number of pros vs. cons.

This activity can be expanded as much as you like. Send students to the library to research trials ahead of time, or to gather newspaper clippings related to the issue. Have them make costumes and courtroom decorations as part of an art project. Videotape the trial or record it with a cassette recorder for future listening and viewing. Have students critique the performances, the arguments, and the decision.

## ESL/LEP ACTIVITY

Write the following words on the board:

*women, men, boys, girls, nurse, doctor, U.S. President, skirt, pants, military, war, stay-at-home parent, chef, flight attendant, football*

Ask the students to write a pro or con statement using some of these words.  Then, have them read their statements to the class. Take a hands vote to see how many classmates agree or disagree with the statements.

## Answer Key

*Checking Your Understanding*
1. b, 2. b, 3. a, 4. c.

*Choosing an Issue*
Answers will vary.

*Getting the Facts*
*Look*

Answers will vary. Possible answers: A girl is winning a race.  Two girls and one boy are racing.  The boy and girl who are not winning are frowning.  The girl breaking the ribbon is smiling. The girl is faster than the boy.

*Listen to Others*

Answers will vary. Discussion should focus on winning and losing.  Possible answers: The boy and girl are playing field hockey.  The boy is wearing a skirt. The boy is serious. The boy is faster than the girl.

*Remember the Facts*
1. At first, George wanted to play football.
2. George doesn't mind putting on the team uniform to play.
3. The school did not offer many sports for George to play.

4. The coach says it's not easy to have a boy on the team.
5. George doesn't play as much as he would like to.
6. George is thinking of quitting the team next spring.

*Ask Questions*
Answers will vary.

*Organizing the Information*
*played with a ball*  baseball, football, basketball, tennis, soccer, golf, handball, racquetball

*played without a ball*  wrestling, ice hockey, swimming, running, cycling, jumping, boxing, badminton

*why it was easy*  He was an excellent player. He was fast. He played street hockey. He was rougher than the girls.

*why it was hard*  He was heckled. He didn't get to play as much as he wanted. He wasn't treated fairly. He had to wear a skirt.

*what happened first*  3, 1, 2

*what happened first in story*  5, 2, 1, 4, 3, 6

*Taking a Closer Look*
*fact and opinion*  1. fact, 2. opinion, 3. fact, 4. opinion, 5. opinion, 6. opinion, 7. fact

*finish each statement*
1. ...he played street hockey as a child
2. ...the rules say you have to wear the uniform in order to play
3. ...the lawyers studied government rules on equal rights and said it was appropriate *or*
   ...girls were allowed to play on city high school football and wrestling teams
4. ...people heckle him, referees are tough on him, he doesn't get to play as much
5. ...he wears a skirt to play

*pros/cons*  1. pro, 2. pro, 3. con, 4. con, 5. con, 6. con

Opinion sentences will vary.

*cause/effect*  2, 1; 1 ,2; 2, 1; 2, 1; 1, 2

*matching*

| | |
|---|---|
| studied equal rights cases | the lawyers |
| confused | the coach |
| determined | George |
| tough | the referees |

*Thinking Other Ways*
Answers will vary.  Possible answers:
1. People would lose the ball a lot.
2. The game would be slower moving.
3. They would shorten periods because players would get too hot.
4. It would be less traumatic for George.

5. More boys would want to join the field hockey team.
6. What if boys and girls could wear whatever they wanted playing sports?
7. The girl would quit because boys play too rough.
8. I would be interested to see how rough George plays.

*Talk about...*
Answers will vary.

*Telling It Your Way*
Answers will vary.

*Think about this...*
Answers will vary.

*Deciding What Is Important*
1-3  Answers will vary

*pros/cons*  Answers will vary.

*answer the question*  Answers will vary.  Suggest that when students answer yes or no to the issues they have selected, they include some facts and opinions from page 10, and some pro and cons from page 11 that support their own opinions, as well as supporting details they found in the story.

*What's your point of view?*
Answers will vary.  Students should now assimilate all facts and opinions from the story, activities, and class discussions to form their own point of view on the issue.  As they present their point of view, they should be able to give supporting details as to why they feel the way they do.  Discuss the different points of view with the class.  Ask students if they changed their minds from what they first thought about the issue.  What made them change their minds?  Do they now see that there is always more than one point of view on an issue?

## ISSUE 2    A Longer School Year?

*Summary:*  Whether the American school year should be lengthened is the issue.  The story discusses the length of some other countries' school years, including Japan and England.  Since students in most other countries spend more days in school per year, one supporting view states that the United States needs to make the school year longer in order for American students to learn as much as students in other nations and to be competitive.  The story also presents some opposing views such as summer vacation being an accepted part of American culture and the fact that it would cost the United States billions of dollars to keep schools open the whole year.  The story also considers the opinions of students, lawmakers, and typical Americans, as represented in a poll.

*Background Information:* This story explores variations in the length of a school year among major industrialized nations. This disparity in length of a school year is a matter of concern for many education policy-makers. Proponents of adding days to an American school year use standardized test scores as evidence for change. Often, American students do not fare as well on assessment devices as students from countries with longer school years. It is assumed by many that increasing the number of days a student attends school will automatically cause a related increase in test performance. While this connection between test scores and length of academic year is not examined in the article, it could be explored through class discussion. Consider the following topics for discussion:

- If there is a link between number of days in school and test performance, what would one expect to find when exploring the scores of students who maintain perfect attendance as compared to students with a high rate of absenteeism?
- What other factors might affect test scores?

## ENRICHMENT ACTIVITY

Role play a meeting of the local Board of Education. Explain to students that the purpose of this meeting is to vote on extending the local school district's academic year from 180 days to 200 days. Appoint five students to the Board to vote. However, before holding a vote, members of the community will be allowed to express their points of view on the issue. Have class members act as the following community members: Sal Smart, president of the high school student council; Mary Merriment, owner of a summer day camp for elementary school students; Mark Score, leader of a community group looking for ways to improve the SAT scores of the town's high school students; and Wanda Worker, a single parent who has to arrange for summer care of her four school age children so that she can work full time.

## ESL/LEP ACTIVITY

As a whole class activity, compile a list of ten questions students would like to ask pupils in another country. Then pair a native English speaker with each ESL/LEP student. Have students use the list of questions to find out about school in the ESL/LEP student's native land. Invite the students to present the results of their interviews to the class.

## Answer Key

*Checking Your Understanding*
1. b, 2. b, 3. b, 4. a

*Choosing an Issue*
Answers will vary.

*Getting the Facts*
*Look*

1. Answers will vary depending on area and school district. Holidays may include, in the order that they occur: Rosh Hashana, Labor Day, Yom Kippur, Columbus Day, Thanksgiving Day (and Friday following), Christmas Eve Day, Christmas Day, New Year's Day, Martin Luther King, Jr. Day, President's Day, Good Friday, Memorial Day. Students may also name Christmas or Winter break, Easter or Spring break, and summer vacation.

2. Answers will vary. Possible answers include:
   September – Rosh Hashana, Labor Day, Yom Kippur
   October – Columbus Day
   November – Thanksgiving Day (and Friday following)
   December – Christmas Eve Day, Christmas Day, Christmas or Winter break
   January – New Year's Day, Martin Luther King, Jr. Day
   February – President's Day
   April – Good Friday, Easter or Spring break
   May – Memorial Day

3. Answers will vary except for fixed holidays, i.e.: Good Friday, Thanksgiving, etc.

4. Answers will vary based on area, religion, etc.

5. Answers will vary based on area, religion, etc.

6. Answers will vary. Accept any reasonable answer. Discuss with students why they chose the answer they did. Have students check to see if their answer is correct.

*holidays that we celebrate* Answers will vary. Possible answers:

1. Cinco de Mayo
2. May
3. Day of week varies each year
4. None

*Listen to others*

Answers will vary. Possible answers include: Traditional holidays such as Rosh Hashana, Yom Kippur, Christmas, Hanukkah, Kwanza

*Remember the Facts*

1. F/Students in England have longer summer vacations than students in Japan.
2. T
3. F/A school year in England is about 192 days. *Or* A school year in Japan is about 243 days.

4. T

5. T

6. F/More than half of Americans polled want to make the school year longer.

*Ask Questions*

1-4 Answers will vary. Help students tally yes and no answers. Teacher could pick one question and poll the entire class.

5-6 Answers will vary. Possible answers include: Do you think the money it would cost to lengthen the school year is worth it? Do you think students need to go to school more days to learn more?

1-6 Answers will vary. Help students tally yes and no answers. Review the meaning of the term majority, and help students decide whether the majority of people answered yes or no to the questions. Suggest that students use this information to answer the next summary question.

*Organizing the Information*

*most important*  Our schools must be equal to schools in other nations.

*less important*  Students in the United States have the shortest school year.

*not very important at all*  Some students like a long summer vacation.

*summer vacation supporting details*  Answers will vary. Look for students using real events, not made-up ones.

*reasons why the school year should be made longer*  B, D, F, G

*reasons why not*  A, C, E, H

*reason agree with most*  Answers will vary. Possible answers: We are all used to a long summer vacation./ Students need summer vacations to work or do summer projects.

*Taking a Closer Look*

1. F, 2. O, 3. O, 4. F, 5. O, 6. O, 7. F, 8. F

*matching reason to opinion*

| | |
|---|---|
| We want students to learn as much as students in other nations. | Then our schools should be equal to other schools in the world. |
| Summer vacation is part of our American culture. | Then we should not take away long summer vacations. |
| Students in America need to learn more. | Then students should spend more time in school. |
| It would cost billions of dollars to increase the school year. | Then the school year should not be made longer. |

*pros/cons*  1. pro, 2. pro, 3. con, 4. pro, 5. con, 6. con, 7. pro

*cause/effect*  a, a, a

*opinions*

(They think) that would be a good idea.

(Some say) if students spend more time in school, they will learn more.

(Those who agree say) that we need a longer school year if we want kids to learn as much as other students.

In fact, we need to make the school year longer.

Our schools should be equal to other schools in the world.

(Some say) we would be asking too much of American students.

(Many think that) it is unfair to students.

We should not expect them to go to school the same number of days as students in other nations.

*I think that students in England and Japan:*  Answers will vary. Students may want to use supporting details from the story to support their opinions.

*Thinking Other Ways*

1. Japan

2. England

3. England/United States

4. United States

5. Answers will vary. Possible answers include: Students in Japan go to school the most number of days per year./Students in the United States go to school fewer days than students in Japan.

*I would like to go to school in...*  Answers will vary. Students should use supporting details from the story to support their opinions.

*Talk about...*

Answers will vary. Help students tally answers.

*Telling It Your Way*

Answers will vary.

*Think about this...*

Answers will vary. Possible answers include:

1. baseball, Independence Day (Fourth of July)

2. Answers will vary.

3. Answers will vary.

*Deciding What Is Important*

1-3 Answers will vary.

4. Answers will vary. Summary should mention that American students spend less time in school, more time in school will equal more learning, and most Americans polled favor increasing the school year.

5. Answers will vary. Summary should mention that lengthening the school year would cost billions, kids would miss summer vacations, and we might be asking too much of students.

*answer the question*  Answers will vary. Suggest that when students answer yes or no to the issues they have selected, they include some pro and cons from page 31 and reasons why the school year should and should not be made longer from page 29 that support their own opinions, as well as supporting details they found in the story.

*What's your point of view?*
Answers will vary. Students should now assimilate all facts and opinions from the story, activities, and class discussions to form their own points of view on the issue. As they present their points of view, they should be able to give supporting details as to why they feel the way they do. Discuss the different points of view with the class. Ask students if they changed their minds from what they first thought about the issue. What made them change their minds? Do they now see that there is always more than one point of view on an issue?

## ISSUE 3    Don't Flunk Lunch!

*Summary:* The story discusses a new plan by the USDA to cut down fat in school lunches. The existing plan follows the meal pattern approach started in the 1940s which requires a meat, vegetable or fruit, a bread, and milk in every lunch. Recent research and studies show that this plan was failing in many schools, resulting in high calorie and fat content in lunches. The new plan aims to reduce salt, fat, and calories for healthier eating. The new plan is based on good judgment. Any lunch can be served as long as it contains the necessary nutrients and is healthy. Opposing views on this new plan are that the computer software that may be needed to analyze lunches would be too expensive and, possibly too difficult, for the existing staff members to use. Therefore, special dieticians would be required or schools might resort to buying prepackaged food  Also, taste and student approval are other concerns.

*Background Information:* A recent survey showed that many meals served in public schools are high in fat content. Learning about good nutrition and changing our eating habits are important. Science has proven that diets high in fat increase the risk of certain ailments such as heart disease. Restricting the amount of fat in one's diet reduces the likelihood of this occurring. In this story, students consider whether serving more nutritious, fat-free lunches in school cafeterias will cause an overall change in people's eating habits. Possible topics for further class discussion:

- Is it the responsibility of a school to "teach" youngsters how to eat properly? Or, should this instruction come from the home? Should students be able to make their own guidelines about how healthy they want to be? Explain.

- How much responsibility should the government assume in prohibiting cigarette smoking? Explain.

## ENRICHMENT ACTIVITY

Have students search their cabinets at home for a copy of the Food Guide Pyramid. The packages of many food products show this guide to daily food choices. The Food Guide Pyramid is a visual model that illustrates how to build a healthful diet by eating a variety of foods each day. Encourage students to use the Food Guide Pyramid to assess the nutritional balance of the foods they consumed yesterday. Then have them use the model to create a balanced meal plan for tomorrow.

## ESL/LEP ACTIVITY

On one set of index cards, write each of the *Words to Know.* Shuffle these cards and place them in a pile face down. On another set of cards, write the definition for each word. Spread the definition cards face up on a flat surface. Have a student draw the top word card. Ask the student to say the term aloud. Challenge the student to match the word card with its definition card.

## Answer Key

*Checking Your Understanding*
1. c,  2. b,  3. a,  4. b

*Choosing an Issue*
Answers will vary.

*Getting the Facts*
*Look*
*Check meal pattern menus*  Monday X;   Tuesday X; Wednesday X; Thursday ✔; Friday X

*Check new plan menus*  Monday X;   Tuesday ✔; Wednesday ✔; Thursday X; Friday ✔

*do not meet USDA guidelines*   Monday and Thursday

*why*  b

*alike/different*  Answers will vary. Students might mention regular milk vs. low fat milk/turkey burger vs. beef burger/less fried food and more salads on days that meet USDA guidelines.

*Listen to others*
Answers will vary. Help students recognize more healthy foods lower in fat, salt, and calories that meet USDA guidelines. Compare lunches eaten at the school cafeteria with lunches students brought from home. Discuss which ones are healthier. Which meals meet USDA guidelines?

*Remember the Facts*
1. 12
2. USDA
3. government

4. 50
5. some people
6. fat

*L is low in fat or salt/X is not*   X, L, L, L, L, X, X, X, X

*Ask Questions*
Answers will vary.

*chart*   Answers will vary.  Possible answers include: low fat yogurt/ads say it tastes like ice cream/yes, I tried it

low salt and fat-free ham/ad says no fat, half the calories, same taste/no, don't believe it could taste as good

*students design ad*   Answers will vary.  Possible answer: Turkey burgers/Taste just like hamburgers with half the fat and calories!

## Organizing the Information

*chart*   Answers will vary.

high fat/low fat

high salt/low salt

a meat, vegetable or fruit, a bread, and milk/any food and portion that is low in fat and calories.

Students may also mention foods:

pepperoni pizza/pizza with low fat cheese

hamburger/turkey burger

potato chips or french fries/baked potato

1. Answers will vary.  Possible answer:  Both plans contain foods that taste good and give students a good lunch.  Students may also use information from menus on page 44.
2. Answers will vary.  Possible answer:  Meal pattern has a meat, vegetable or fruit, a bread, and milk and USDA new plan has any food and portion that is low in fat and calories.  Students may also use information from previous chart on page 48.
3. new USDA plan would be healthier
4. Answers will vary.  Answers should include that foods would be lower in fat, salt, and calories.  If students chose meal pattern approach, review why new USDA plan would be healthier.

*label food on tray 1*   all healthy

*label food on tray 2*   all not healthy except salad

*analyze tray 1*   yes; foods are lower in fat, salt, and calories

*analyze tray 2*   no; foods are high in fat, salt, and calories (also sugar) except for salad

## Taking a Closer Look

1. ~~more~~/less
2. ~~increase~~/reduce
3. ~~juice~~/milk
4. ~~higher~~/lower
5. ~~high~~/low

*choose any fact*   Answers will vary.

*think about fact*   Answers will vary.

*matching point of view*

| | |
|---|---|
| They feel that improving the nutrition of school meals is their national health responsibility. | USDA |
| They say that the plans are unrealistic. | People |
| They feel they will need some help to follow the new guidelines. | Schools |
| They might say they won't like how the food tastes. | Students |
| It said that many schools did not meet the USDA guidelines | Survey |
| They say that there are a lot of good reasons for kids to eat healthier. | Dieticians |

*pros/cons*   con, con, con, pro, pro, pro

## Thinking Other Ways

*menu*   Answers will vary.

1. Answers will vary.  Possible answers include: cupcakes, cake, cookies, soda, potato chips, candy, etc.
2. Answers will vary.  Help students recognize which foods on their menus are *not* healthy, ie: junk food.
3. Answers will vary.  Help students recognize which foods on their menus are healthy, ie: not junk food.
4. Answers will vary.
5. Answers will vary.  Students should be able to use the standards they have learned about the USDA guidelines of low fat, salt, and calories.  If students plan unhealthy menus, discuss some implications of unhealthy eating like low energy or disease.

*class menu*   Help students create a week's menu that contains healthy foods that are low in fat, salt, and calories, but that still tastes good.  Ask students to mention some of the healthy items that they included in the menus they made themselves on page 53.  Have students ask classmates if they would like to include those items on the class menu.  Ask students if they would like to submit the menu to the school cafeteria or principal as part of a "health week" at school.

## Talk about…

Answers will vary.  Help students tally votes.  Review the term majority that students learned in Issue 2.  Explain that the answer that received the most votes got the majority of votes and discuss why.

## Telling It Your Way

Answers will vary.  Students should include the information they have learned up to this point.  Encourage them to go back to the story or review activities if they need to refresh their memories.  Students should have enough information to support their answer with details.

## Think about this…

Answers will vary.  Possible answers include:  it's hard to break bad eating habits/healthy food doesn't taste as good/don't have access to healthy food

*Deciding What Is Important*
1-3   Answers will vary

*agree and disagree*   Answers will vary.

*answer the question*   Answers will vary. Suggest that when students answer yes or no to the issues they have selected, they include some pro and cons and different points of view from page 52 that support their own opinions, as well as supporting details they found in the story.

*What's your point of view?*
Answers will vary. Students should now assimilate all facts and opinions from the story, activities, and class discussions to form their own points of view on the issue. As they present their points of view, they should be able to give supporting details as to why they feel the way they do. Discuss the different points of view with the class. Ask students if they changed their minds from what they first thought about the issue. What made them change their minds? Do they now see that there is always more than one point of view on an issue?

**Section 3**

# WHAT'S YOUR POINT OF VIEW ON COMMUNITY ISSUES?

## ISSUE 1     Does Every Vote Count?

*Summary:* The story discusses the importance of voting and the fact that so few Americans actually take advantage of this very important right. The story talks about voting opportunities and laws in other countries. In most countries, many people vote because they want to, however, in some countries people vote because they risk persecution. The story discusses the fact that some Americans have had to overcome many obstacles to earn the right to vote. Every vote counts and the story makes this clear. It is important for people to have their say and to make a difference. Some reasons why people may not vote include Tuesday being an inconvenient day to vote, difficulty in registering, and loss of faith in the political system.

*Background Information*   The story presents the fact that only about fifty percent of registered voters participated in the 1988 presidential election. It should be noted that there has never been 100 percent voter participation in any American election. One of the highest voter turnouts ever occurred in the 1960 presidential election when roughly 63% of all registered voters cast ballots to decide between John F. Kennedy and Richard Nixon. Topics for additional discussion:

- In 1971, the voting age was lowered from twenty-one to eighteen. Do you think the percentage of eligible voters who used their right to vote increased or declined in the election of 1972? (It actually declined. About 61 percent of eligible voters cast their ballots in the election of 1968 while only 55 percent of voters cast ballots in the election of 1972.)
- What are some incentives that might cause more Americans to use their right to vote?

## ENRICHMENT ACTIVITY

Have students work in small groups to create a pamphlet that encourages voters to exercise their right to vote. In the pamphlet, students should give factual evidence that supports the idea that every vote *does* count. Pamphlets might also include a description of how a person can register to vote in the community.

## ESL/LEP ACTIVITY

ESL students new to the United States will likely be unfamiliar with the election system. In order to fully grasp the nature of this issue, these youngsters will need some background information on the election process. Pair each ESL/LEP student with a native English speaker. Have the native speaker explain the following words: candidate, citizen, democracy, election, register, voter. Assess the ESL/LEP student's understanding of the process by having each student list ways that the American election system differs from the way officials in their native land attain office.

## Answer Key

*Checking Your Understanding*
1. a, 2. c, 3. b, 4. a

*Choosing an Issue*
Answers will vary.

*Getting the Facts*
*Look*
Answers will vary. Possible answers include: a school council election is going on/a girl candidate is running /a boy candidate is running/audience members are carrying campaign signs

*Listen to others*
Answers will vary. Students should discuss the different things they see happening. Help student explain things they see happening to other students who don't understand campaigns and elections. As a class, students should be able to find three things that they all agree are happening.

*Remember the Facts*

1. F/Any American who is 18 or older can register to vote.
2. T
3. T
4. F/In 1860, only white men were allowed to vote.
5. F/Only registered voters are allowed to vote on Election Day.
6. F/Some people want to hold elections on weekends.

*Ask Questions*

*chart-want to know*   Answers will vary. Possible answers include:

How does an American register to vote?

Why did only half of eligible voters vote in 1988?

What things are important to Americans today?

How can we make it more convenient to vote?

What does a single vote do?

## Organizing the Information

*chart*

*responsibilities*   Answers will vary. Possible answers include: drive safely/have insurance/follow rules of the road/maintain car/get car inspected

*benefits*   allowed to drive/driver's license is valid identification/freedom to go anywhere/less dependent on other people to get around

*chart*

*responsible for*   Answers will vary. Possible answers include: keeping books in good shape/returning books on time/keeping quiet in the library/taking responsibility for books if I lend them to friends

*benefits*   borrow books when I want/use research facilities/study in the library/loan books to friends

*home responsibilities*   Answers will vary. Help students see the positive and negative qualities of their responsibility.

## Taking a Closer Look

*fact/opinion*   1. fact, 2. opinion, 3. fact, 4. fact, 5. opinion, 6. fact, 7. opinion

*make it a fact*

1. ...register to vote.
2. ...the right to vote.
3. ...their citizens vote.
4. ...affect something important to them.
5. ...went to the polls.

*pros/cons*   1. pro, 2. con, 3. pro, 4. con, 5. con, 6. pro, 7. pro

*look at the pros and cons*   Answers will vary.

*cause/effect*   1, 2; 2, 1; 2, 1; 2, 1; 2, 1

*write your own cause/effect*   Answers will vary. Possible answer: People do not vote.

## Thinking Other Ways

Answers will vary. Possible answers:

1. many accidents
2. more people would vote
3. no, even less people would vote
4. more people would vote because it would be more convenient
5. some citizens might move
6. what would happen if everyone voted?

7-8 Students should try to support their answers with facts and opinions from the story.

## Talk about…

Answers will vary. Ask students if they know anyone who lives in one of the countries mentioned in the story.

## Telling It Your Way

Answers will vary. Students should include the information they have learned up to this point. Encourage them to go back to the story or review activities if they need to refresh their memories. Students should have enough information to support their answer with details.

## Think about this…

Answers will vary. Assist students by providing additional background information on women's rights and voting. Help them to imagine the way women and minorities felt when only white men could vote.

## Deciding What Is Important

1-3   Answers will vary

*pros/cons*   Answers will vary.

*answer the question*   Answers will vary. Suggest that when students answer yes or no to the issues they have selected, they include some pro and cons from page 11 and facts and opinions from page 10 that support their own opinions, as well as supporting details they found in the story.

## What's your point of view?

Answers will vary. Students should now assimilate all facts and opinions from the story, activities, and class discussions to form their own points of view on the issue. As they present their points of view, they should be able to give supporting details why they feel the way they do. Discuss the different points of view with the class. Ask students if they changed their minds from what they first thought about the issue. What made them change their minds? Do they now see that there is always more than one point of view on an issue?

# *Tell us what you think!*

Dear Valued Customer,

Thank you for choosing Globe Fearon to be part of your students' success story! To ensure that we continue to meet your needs professionally and in the classroom, we'd like your feedback.

1. What is the title of the text/series in which you received this card?

_______________________________________________

2. For which course/courses are you using this text/series?

_______________________________________________

3. Check the box below that best indicates your satisfaction on each of the factors listed.

| | Completely Satisfied | Somewhat Satisfied | Not at all Satisfied |
|---|---|---|---|
| Adaptable to My Classroom | ❏ | ❏ | ❏ |
| Appropriate Interest Level | ❏ | ❏ | ❏ |
| Motivational | ❏ | ❏ | ❏ |
| Relevant to Students | ❏ | ❏ | ❏ |
| Instructionally Sound | ❏ | ❏ | ❏ |
| Right Combination of Skills and Practice | ❏ | ❏ | ❏ |
| Teacher Support Materials | ❏ | ❏ | ❏ |
| Focus on Life-Skills, Job-Skills, Survival-Skills | ❏ | ❏ | ❏ |

3. What do you like most about this text/series? *(please be specific)*

_______________________________________________

_______________________________________________

4. What would you improve about this text/series? *(please be specific)*

_______________________________________________

_______________________________________________

5. Did you receive the materials in a timely manner?

YES ❏          NO ❏

6. Are there any topics or themes that you would like included in future products to better meet your needs?

_______________________________________________

_______________________________________________

Personal: *(please print neatly)*

❏ Dr.          ❏ Mr.          ❏ Mrs.          ❏ Ms.

First Name ______________________ Last Name ______________________

School Name/Site______________________________________________

Address ______________________________________________

City ______________________ State __________ Zip ______________

Phone ______________________________________________

May we call on you for a testimonial? ______________________________

_______________________________________________

Thank you again for selecting our products and for taking the time to give us your thoughts. If there is any way we can be of assistance to you, please call us at 1-800-848-9500.

# *New from Globe Fearon*

## Person-to-Person
Teaches the social skills students need to succeed in school, at home, and on the job!
Reading Level: 2-3

## The Active Learning Program
A four-book program that teaches key curricula topics in an activity-based setting!
Reading Level: 2-3

## Problem Solving Strategies
Enables students to develop the
problem solving strategies they need in a variety of real life settings!
Reading Level: 3

## Everyday Health
Teaches real-world health through real-world, workplace applications!
Reading Level: 3-4

## What's Your Point of View?
A four-book program that teaches critical thinking skills!
Reading Level: 2-4



## American Expressions
An anthology for integrated learning!
Reading Level: 3-4

## Janus Life Skills
A new 8-book program based on the popular Janus Survival Guides!
Reading Level: 3

## Survival Vocabulary:
## Computer Hardware and Computer Software
Two new worktexts that teach key computer vocabulary!
Reading Level: Below 3

## Money Matters Guides
An 8-book program designed to help students learn money management strategies!
Reading Level: 2.5

For more information on these and other programs,
contact your local representative by calling us toll-free today at
**1-800-848-9500.**

GLOBE FEARON
*Your Partner in Meeting Special Needs*

## BUSINESS REPLY MAIL
FIRST CLASS MAIL    PERMIT NO. 4   UPPER SADDLE RIVER, NJ

POSTAGE WILL BE PAID BY ADDRESSEE

### GLOBE FEARON
ATTN: PRODUCT MARKETING
One Lake Street
Upper Saddle River, NJ 07458-9957

## ISSUE 2    Buckle Up For Safety!

*Summary:* The issue discusses the importance of wearing seat belts, seat belt laws, and the debate about which seat belt law is better—primary or secondary. The story names reasons why people should *always* wear seat belts: three out of four accidents happen within 25 miles of a person's home; most accidents happen when a car isn't going very fast; and when people wear seat belts there are fewer fatalities. These are good reasons why people should wear seat belts even if they are driving around the corner. The story also discusses reasons why people do not wear their seat belts: seat belts are too much trouble; if you use air bags, you don't need to buckle up; if a car is moving slowly you won't get into an accident; and if a car goes underwater you are safer without your seat belt. The point is made that seat belts save lives. Given that, what lengths should we go to to require people to wear seat belts?

*Background Information:* In this article, students discover that wearing safety belts saves lives. They explore reasons why people would choose to disregard this fact and ride without a belt. Students might be interested to discover that motor-vehicle accidents are the greatest cause of accident deaths in the United States each year. More than one half of all motor vehicle deaths occurred in night accidents. In 1991, about half of all traffic fatalities involved an alcohol-impaired driver or non-occupant. Using this data as a base, additional topics for discussion include:

- Suppose roads were closed between 9 PM and 6 AM. What effect might this have on motor-vehicle accidents?

- What is the current penalty a driver incurs if found driving while intoxicated? Do you think this penalty is just? Or, should it be changed? Explain.

## ENRICHMENT ACTIVITY

Explain to students that motor vehicle regulations are determined by state governments. As such, the rules and regulations vary from state to state. Challenge groups of students to use reference texts to determine the state which has the youngest beginning driver age, the oldest beginning driver age, the lowest highway speed limit, and the greatest highway speed limit.

## ESL/LEP ACTIVITY

Write the word *violation* on the board. Underline the suffix *-ion*. Tell students that this suffix means "the state of " or "the act of". Write the word *violate* next to violation on the board. Have students use a dictionary to find the meaning of this word. Develop the idea that both terms come from the same base word and have related meanings. *Violate* means to break the law. *Violation* means the act of breaking the law. Challenge students to use the skills they learned to determine the relationship between *inflate* and *inflation*.

## Answer Key

*Checking Your Understanding*
1. b, 2. c, 3. a, 4. b

*Choosing an Issue*
Answers will vary.

*Getting the Facts*
*Look*
1. show how to put on a seat belt
2. put the clip in the buckle until you hear a click
3. push the button on the buckle (to release the clip)
*circle answer*   1. b, 2. c, 3. a

*Listen to others*
Answers will vary. Students should be able to find all the reasons in the story. As a class, see if students can think of some other reasons why people do or don't wear seat belts.

*Remember the Facts*
1. F/Many accidents happen even when a car isn't going very fast.
2. F/Many accidents happen close to home.
3. T
4. T
5. T
6. F/Nine states have a primary safety belt law. Also accept: All fifty states have child-safety belt laws.

*Ask Questions*
*chart-how to find out*   Answers will vary. Possible answers include: talk to someone at the local police station/interview people I know

*independent research*   Answers will vary.

*Organizing the Information*
*reasons why riders wear seat belts*
They feel safe.

Seat belts protect them from being thrown forward.

Air bags alone are not enough.

Accidents often happen close to home.

Seat belts save lives.

Wearing seat belts is the law.

*reasons why riders do not wear seat belts*

Seat belts are too much trouble to use.

If you use air bags, you don't need to buckle up.

If a car is moving slowly you won't get into an accident.

If a car goes underwater you are safer without your seat belt. (Seat belts trap you.)

*reasons why riders wear seat belts*   A, B, D, G

*reasons why riders do not wear seat belts*   C, E, F, H

*choose most important reason*   Answers will vary.

## Taking a Closer Look

*fact/opinion*   1. fact,   2. fact,   3. opinion,   4. opinion, 5. opinion, 6. opinion, 7. opinion, 8. fact

*column 1/column 2*

1. mandatory/children must always wear seat belts
2. debate/a heated discussion in state legislatures about seat belt laws
3. fatalities/the number of people killed in car accidents
4. inflate/air bags filling up in a crash

*pros/cons*   1. pro, 2. pro, 3. con, 4. con, 5. con, 6. pro

*finding supporting details*

Three out of four accidents happen within 25 miles of a person's home.

Many accidents happen even when a car isn't going very fast.

More than 80% of accidents happen when people are driving less than 40 miles per hour.

When people wear seat belts, there are fewer fatalities.

Seat belts save lives.

Air bags are designed to be used with seat belts.

Air bags inflate only in front-end crashes.

They do not inflate in rear or side crashes.

Air bags won't help you if you're in the back seat.

It is not true that you are safer without a seat belt if your car catches fire or goes underwater.

Seat belts keep you from hitting your head.

Seat belts help you help yourself to safety.

## Thinking Other Ways

Answers will vary.  Possible answers:

1. more people might wear seat belts
2. people could get a discount on car insurance

*seat belts on buses*   Answers will vary.  Students supporting seat belts on buses should use pros from page 31 as well as information from the story.  Students not supporting seat belts on buses should use cons from page 31 as well as information from the story.

*police officers*   may think they can't get in and out of the car fast enough

*old cars with no seat belts*   may have to get new cars, have seat belts put in, or risk danger, and getting tickets

*don't like seat belts*   risk danger and risk getting tickets

## Talk about…

Answers will vary.  Ask students if they have ever worn a seat belt on a bus.  How did they feel?  If not, how would it make them feel?  Students should support their answers with safety issues.

## Telling It Your Way

Answers will vary.  Students should include the information they have learned up to this point.  Encourage them to go back to the story or review activities if they need to refresh their memories.  Students should have enough information to support their answer with details.

## Think about this…

Answers will vary.

## Deciding What Is Important

1-3   Answers will vary.

*pros/cons*   Answers will vary.

*answer the question*   Answers will vary.  Suggest that when students answer yes or no to the issues they have selected, they include some facts they included on the spider chart on page 28, pro and cons from page 31, and facts and opinions from page 30 that support their own opinions, as well as supporting details they found in the story.

## What's your point of view?

Answers will vary.  Students should now assimilate all facts and opinions from the story, activities, and class discussions to form their own points of view on the issue.  As they present their points of view, they should be able to give supporting details why they feel the way they do.  Discuss the different points of view with the class.  Ask students if they changed their minds from what they first thought about the issue.  What made them change their minds?  Do they now see that there is always more than one point of view on an issue?

## ISSUE 3   The American Way

*Summary:*   The story introduces the concept of civic-mindedness.  It discusses the importance of the American Way and the fact that Americans today seem to have lost the willingness to participate in community events and work together to improve the places in which they live.  The issue mentions three main reasons why people may not participate as much as they used to in community activities: they feel that their participation will not make a difference; more women work outside the home than ever before, therefore, they no longer have the time many women once had for volunteering; and they think it is the government's job to take care of things and make changes. That is, many people feel that they are fulfilling their civic duty simply by voting. They think that if they vote to get the right people in office then it is the government's job to promote change The story lists many reasons why civic-mindedness is crucial in our working society. It is the American Way that has made America what it is today.

*Background Information:* This issue explores possible reasons why Americans seem to be unwilling to participate in community events. In the past, Americans had to work together to create new cities and towns. The survival of community members often depended upon community support.

However, today there seems to be less of a willingness and need to work together. Perhaps this is due to the fact that people's lives are not dependent upon such cooperation. Today community involvement means making a town a "better place to live" rather than making sure the townspeople "can continue to live." This difference could be further explored through the following topic:

- It seems that Americans volunteer to participate in community affairs when people's lives are at risk. Why might this be the case?

## ENRICHMENT ACTIVITY

Divide the class into groups of three or four students. Have each group decide what it thinks is the biggest community problem. Then, write a letter to someone in the Office of the Mayor or Town Council, or to the state government, voicing concern and asking for suggestions on how to help remedy the problem. Groups should share their findings with the class by creating a poster encouraging community members to be aware of the problem.

## ESL/LEP ACTIVITY

Students may have difficulty grasping the notion of a "community". Review the definition of this term expressed in the *Words to Know* section. Tell students that there are many different kinds of communities. One community is the place where you live. But a community can also be a group of people who share common traits or work for a common cause. Ask students to identify some communities that they belong to. Possible answers include a community of students, a community of teens, a sports community, or a community that enjoys the music of a particular entertainer, etc.

## Answer Key

*Checking Your Understanding*
1. c, 2. b, 3. a, 4. c

*Choosing an Issue*
Answers will vary.

*Getting the Facts*
*Look*
Answers will vary. Possible answers include freedom, peace, unity, USA, American-made

*Listen to others*
Answers will vary. Answers should mention freedom, and other ideas that are associated with the United States of America. Other symbols may include the recycle symbol, hearing-impaired symbol, Girl Scouts/Boy Scouts symbol.

*Remember the Facts*
1. F/The American Way is when American people help each other.
2. F/Americans are less civic-minded than ever before.
3. T
4. F/People, not the government, will make communities better.
5. F/More American women work now than ever before.
6. F/Working together will strengthen community ties.

*Ask Questions*

✔ *equals helpful/X equals not helpful at all*   1. ✔, 2. X, 3. ✔, 4. X, 5. ✔, 6. ✔, 7. ✔, 8. X, 9. ✔

*one more question*   Answers will vary. Possible answer: What was the last thing you did to help your community, and when did you do it?

*Organizing the Information*

*not supporting details*
We all live in a community.
It is up to the government to make a community work.
The government should not stop women from working.

*putting things in order*
1. The storm blew the farmer's barn away.
2. The farmer began to build a new barn.
3. The neighbors helped the farmer finish building the new barn.

*putting events from the story in order*
1. In the past, American people worked together to build farms, towns and cities.
2. At one time, housewives did a lot of volunteer work.
3. Many people no longer have a lot of time to get involved in community activities.
4. Americans today are not civic-minded anymore.

*Taking a Closer Look*
1. ~~government~~/community, 2. ~~government~~/people,
3. ~~worse~~/better, 4. ~~men~~/women, 5. ~~workers~~/women

*fact/opinion* Answers will vary. Possible answer: *(fact)* More women work now than ever before. *(opinion)* I think that both men and women should put in equal amounts of volunteer work since both now work outside the home.

*pros/cons* 1. con, 2. pro, 3. con, 4. con, 5. pro, 6. pro

*writing opinions* Answers will vary. Possible answer: *(pros)* People should be more civic-minded because it takes more than just electing the right people to government positions in order to make our communities better—it takes people. Working together as a community helps people learn to solve problems (before they become a crisis), and helps people develop leadership skills.

*(cons)* I think it is difficult for the government to require all people to volunteer to make communities better because some people think it is the government's job to make communities better. Also, people do not have a lot of free time and may not be able to volunteer. People even think that if they did find time to volunteer, it wouldn't make a difference anyway.

*supporting details*

They don't think this job is their responsibility.

They think it is only their obligation to vote.

If they vote for the right people to run the government, then these people will take care of everything.

Today, people don't feel that community involvement is important.

They say it is up to the government to make our communities work and to make our communities better.

Another reason why there is less involvement is because more women work now than ever before.

In the past, many volunteers in community activities were housewives.

They had more time to get involved in their community.

Today, a lot of people do not have a lot of extra time to get involved in community activities.

*kinds of things* Answers will vary. Possible answers include:

People need to remember that communities are made better by the people who live in them.

People can work together to help each other and make their communities better places to live.

People could donate a set number of hours per week or month to a community cause.

People could plan community events so people will feel good about their communities and participate.

*cause/effect* 1, 2; 2, 1; 1, 2; 2, 1; 2, 1

*others* Answers will vary. Possible answer:

*cause* People wanted to do more than just vote to make their communities better.

*effect* Communities improved.

**20**

*Thinking Other Ways*
Answers will vary. Possible answers:

1. They like it because it helps make their community a nice place.
2. It is a nice community where everyone solves problems and works together.
3. Many people will want to move there and the population will increase.
4. Yes, because everyone has to volunteer the same amount of time for a good cause.

*explore the issues* Answers will vary. Possible answers:
1. People who had no time for community work might not vote.
2. If someone contributed a certain number of hours to a "community project" that person could receive the same number of hours in return from the community for a project of his or her own, like building a shed.
3. You could volunteer to support a person running for town office by helping with the campaign.

*Talk about...*
Answers will vary. Students should include the concepts obedience and civility in their definition of a good American citizen—someone who follows the laws and rules of the country. As a citizen we have the right to vote, freedom, etc. We have the responsibility to follow the laws, defend our country, etc. As a community we have the right to make it a nice place to live, to elect and/or run for county government, vote for the right, qualified candidate for county government, etc. Students should use details from the story and ideas talked about in class for ways to make their community a better place to live.

*Telling It Your Way*
Answers will vary. Students should include the information they have learned up to this point. Encourage them to go back to the story or review activities if they need to refresh their memories. Students should have enough information to support their answer with details.

*Think about this...*
Answers will vary.

*Deciding What Is Important*
1-3 Answers will vary.

*pros/cons* Answers will vary.

*answer the question* Answers will vary. Suggest that when students answer yes or no to the issues they have selected, they include some facts from pages 44 and 48, and some pros and cons from page 49 that support their own opinions, as well as supporting details they found on page 50 from the story.

*What's your point of view?*
Answers will vary. Students should now assimilate all facts and opinions from the story, activities, and class discussions to form their own points of view on the issue. As

they present their points of view, they should be able to give supporting details as to why they feel the way they do. Discuss the different points of view with the class. Ask students if they changed their minds from what they first thought about the issue. What made them change their minds? Do they now see that there is always more than one point of view on an issue?



# WHAT'S YOUR POINT OF VIEW ON THE ENVIRONMENT?

## ISSUE 1  The Cleanup Kids

*Summary:* The story discusses all the things that young people do to help clean up the environment, and to help protect wildlife. Kids everywhere are joining the cleanup and they are asking for help from everybody, even the government. Some people are urging the government to protect animals from illegal hunting, to save the forests for natural habitats, and to stop pollution. However, the government says it can't force people to clean up and that it may be more important for money to go to people instead of to protecting the animals. The main issue is responsibility. Should it be the responsibility of the government to protect our environment? We all have the right to a clean, beautiful world, but should we all then be prepared to pitch in?

*Background Information:* This story describes various ways that young people work to protect the environment. Many students think of environment awareness as being restricted to reducing pollution. However, it is equally important that the natural environments of animal populations are maintained. Many animal species have become endangered or even extinct due to human interference of their habitats. The World Resources Institute predicts that if current trends continue about one-fourth of all plant and animal species existing in the mid-1980's will become extinct within 25 years. Topics for further class discussion on this issue include:

- Forests are natural habitats for thousands of plants and animals. Humans cut down trees for products used in their daily lives. Currently, some forests are restricted and kept as natural preserves for plants and animals. What would be the effects of preserving greater forest areas?

- If the amount of restricted forest areas is increased, the supply of wood will decrease. This will cause an increase in the cost of products made from trees. How would this change the supply and demand of products made of wood?

## ENRICHMENT ACTIVITY

Have students think about what an animal might say to his human neighbors about the need to protect the environment. Ask each student to create a poster that illustrates a message from Earth's animals to Earth's humans. Some students may prefer to create a poem or rap song to spread the message!

## ESL/LEP ACTIVITY

Write the words *abandoned* and *recycling* on the board. Tell students that both words are action words. Endings show when the action occurred—in the past, in the present, or in the future. Ask a volunteer to name the ending in the first word. Develop the idea that the ending *-ed* shows that the action happened in the past. Ask another volunteer to name the ending in the second word. Develop the idea that the ending *-ing* shows that the action is happening presently. Challenge students to name the form of the word *abandon* that shows the action is happening presently (abandoning). Then have them name the form of the word *recycle* that shows the action happened in the past (recycled). You may extend the activity by having students add these endings to the other verbs in the *Words to Know* list.

## Answer Key

*Checking Your Understanding*
1. b,  2 .a,  3. b,  4. c

*Choosing an Issue*
Answers will vary.

*Getting the Facts*
*Look*
Answers will vary.

1. newspapers, glass, metal, plastic jugs, tin cans
2. newspapers not tied with string, dirty metal cans, tin cans not flattened
3. Monday
4. they must be tied with string
5. Sunday

*Listen to others*
1. F/Young people are thinking about the environment and making it a better place to live.
2. T
3. F/In 1994, $50,000 worth of pennies was collected for the Children's Earth Fund.
4. F/The government wants to spend more money on people. *Or*
   The government wants to spend less money on animals.)

*ask questions*
*glass*   I know that I have to throw it away in a separate trash can./What would happen if I didn't?

*newspapers*   I know that newspapers can be recycled into other papers./How do they do that?

*tin cans*   I know that tin cans are usually separated from other recyclables, like metal cans./Why?

*car tires*   I know that sometimes I see them piled up high at the town dump./What happens to them after that?

*metal*   I know they have to be flattened before I bring them for recycling./What if I can't flatten them before I bring them?

*Organizing the Information*

cycle map

1. the water cycle
2. it falls to the earth
3. warm air
4. clouds begin to form

*symbol*   Answers will vary.  Possible answers:

1. It moves clockwise and ends up back at the beginning.
2. because recycling is when we take something, use it, and then turn it back into another usable form
3. it symbolizes reusing, saving the environment, a complete process
4. newspapers, boxes, bottles

*Taking a Closer Look*

*fact/opinion*   1. opinion, 2. fact, 3. fact, 4. fact, 5. opinion, 6. opinion, 7. opinion, 8. opinion

*finish each statement*

1. …she didn't like the litter that was piling up.
2. …they want to make their communities more beautiful.
3. …more money should be spent on people instead.  *Or* …it is too costly.
4. …we all have that right.

*pros/cons*   1. pro, 2. pro, 3. pro, 4. con, 5. pro, 6. pro

*why is it a good idea*   Answers will vary. Possible answer: It is a good idea for the government to require people to join the clean up because the government must protect animals from being hunted illegally, save the forests for natural habitats, and stop pollution. Planting trees and gardens will make our communities more beautiful. Finally, pollution must be stopped in some way so everyone needs to pitch in.

*why is it not a good idea*   Answers will vary. Possible answer:  It is not a good idea for the government to require people to clean up because people should not be forced to do something they do not want to do. Plus, the government should spend any extra money they have on the problems that people have, not animals.

*cause/effect*   2, 1; 1, 2; 2, 1; 1, 2; 2, 1

*column 2*   2, 3, 1, 5, 4

*Thinking Other Ways*

1. Answers will vary. Possible answer: Recycling would be even more difficult than it is now, and harder to get people to do.
2. Answers will vary.  Possible answer: Trash would just pile up and destroy wildlife and the environment.
3. Answers will vary.  Possible answer:  All people might not be happy, but the environment would be cleaner and wildlife would be safer and the forests could be preserved as habitats.
4. Answers will vary.  Possible answer:  One of them might tell us that he needs help because the animals can't save themselves.
5. Answers will vary.  Possible answer:  I could join a save an animal organization and try to get others to join as well.
6. Answers will vary.

*graph*

1. 1965
2. 75 million tons
3. it has increased

*Talk about…*

Answers will vary.  Possible answer:  The amount of garbage we are making is increasing every year.  If we don't start cutting down now, or at least changing our habits, the condition of our environment will begin to decline and eventually our air won't be clean and our forests and wild life will be deteriorated.

*Telling It Your Way*

*graph*   2, 1, 3, 4

*Think about this…*

Answers will vary.

*Deciding What Is Important*

1-3   Answers will vary.

*pros/cons*   Answers will vary.

*answer the question*   Answers will vary.  Suggest that when students answer yes or no to the issues they have selected, they include some facts and opinions from page 10, and some pros and cons from page 11 that support their own opinions, as well as supporting details they found in the story.

*What's your point of view?*

Answers will vary.  Students should now assimilate all facts and opinions from the story, activities, and class discussions to form their own points of view on the issue. As they present their points of view, they should be able to give supporting details as to why they feel the way they do.  Discuss the different points of view with the class. Ask students if they changed their minds from what they first thought about the issue.  What made them change their minds?  Do they now see that there is always more than one point of view on an issue?

# ISSUE 2    What's in the Water?

*Summary:* The issue focuses on the condition of our nation's water systems, the evolution of the Clean Water Act, and our growing awareness of the problem of water pollution. The issue also talks about point and nonpoint pollution and discusses potential ways to fight both. However, with all the reformation and effort being put forth, nonpoint pollution is still a major problem. One problem is that in order to fight nonpoint pollution, many hard-working people may have to suffer, such as farmers and builders. Farmers would have to change crops, plow less, and stop using bug sprays. This would result in smaller crops and less money for the farmers. Building codes could be changed to reduce nonpoint pollution, but this could result in added costs for builders, which would amount to added costs for home buyers. Many young people are trying to save our water, but is that enough? The issue focuses on responsibility. We all want to have clean water, but what are we willing to give up in the process?

*Background Information:* This story explores the problem of water pollution and describes efforts to reduce the contamination of our nations' rivers and lakes. Conservation of Earth's freshwater supply is vital to all living things. Although roughly three-fourths of the Earth is covered with water, about 97% of it is salt water. Much of the remaining 3% is freshwater that exists as ice in the polar regions. As a result, a very small amount of freshwater is suited for use by living things. Yet, all living things need water to survive! An additional topic for discussion regarding this issue:

- If the government places restrictions on farmers' crop production, how might this affect pollution?

## ENRICHMENT ACTIVITY

Divide the class into groups of three or four students. Ask each group to create a public service announcement that educates the public about the need to conserve Earth's water. Have the groups use a tape recorder to tape their messages. Share the recordings with the class.

## ESL/LEP ACTIVITY

Review the *Words to Know* with the students. Challenge them to identify a relationship that exists between each of the following pairs of words: sewage, point pollution; runoff, nonpoint pollution; fertilizers, algae.

## Answer Key

*Checking Your Understanding*

1. b, 2. c, 3. a, 4. b

*Choosing an Issue*
Answers will vary.

*Getting the Facts*
look

*freshwater*   Of, relating to, living in, or consisting of water that is not salty.

*saltwater*   Relating to, consisting of, or containing salt water.

*stagnant*   Not moving or flowing; motionless; Foul or stale from standing.

*rainwater*   Water that has fallen as rain.

*purify*   To rid of impurities; to clean.

*Listen to others*   Answers will vary.

*Remember the facts*
1. F/Before 1972, rivers and lakes were in terrible condition.
2. F/The Clean Water Act helped fight point pollution.
3. T
4. F/Stopping pollution is difficult because it comes from many places.

*ask questions*
Answers will vary.

*Organizing the Information*
*flow chart*
*left*   factories
*middle*   fertilizers
*right*   bathrooms, wastes
*rainwater flow chart*   runoff, streams, rivers, oceans

1. the flow of rain water
2. It flows in procession explaining what happens to something.
3. Answers will vary.

*things that would stop water pollution*   A, B, E, G

*things that would cause water pollution*   C, D, F, H

*Taking a Closer Look*
*fact/opinion*   1. fact, 2. fact, 3. fact, 4. opinion, 5. opinion, 6. fact, 7. opinion, 8. fact

*column 2*   3, 5, 1, 2, 4

*pros/cons*   1. pro, 2. con, 3. pro, 4. pro, 5. con, 6. pro

*why it is a good idea*   Answers will vary. Possible answer: It is a good idea for the government to require people to reduce pollution because before the Clean Water Act which made polluting illegal, our rivers and lakes were in poor condition. Even today, some students are finding that the stream they adopted is polluted. Some farmers do not care how much bug spray they use because they want to have more crops and earn more money. But bug spray and fertilizers pollute our waters. Too much fertilizer and animal wastes in lakes can cause algae, and algae kills fish.

*why it is difficult*   Answers will vary. Possible answer: It is difficult for the government to require people to reduce pollution because people should not be forced to do something they do not want to do. Plus, nonpoint pollution is too difficult to control because it comes from so many sources. Finally, forcing builders to follow tough building codes would make the price of buying a home too costly. Then, homebuyers would suffer because they couldn't afford to buy new houses.

*jar 1*   The paper towel is clean.

*jar 2*   The paper towel is dirty.

*jar 3*   b. Beads of oil will float across the water. The oil will stick to the paper towel. c. It's hard to do because oil floats on water.

### Thinking Other Ways

1. Answers will vary. Possible answer: The oil would spread all over the ocean, killing animals, and destroying the plant life.
2. Answers will vary. Possible answer: The ocean would be polluted and plant and animal life would suffer.

*what we can do to save water*

1. Answers will vary. Any of the nine answers on the list are acceptable.
2. Answers will vary. Any of the nine answers on the list are acceptable.
3. Answers will vary. Possible answer: We all need water to live.

*what we can do to save water*

1. taking a bath
2. Less water is used when taking a short shower.
3. Answers will vary.

### Talk about…

Answers will vary. Have students read labels of some foods they eat. Assist them in locating water in the list of ingredients. Explain to students that if our water was polluted, it would not only be in our baths and pools, but especially in things that we eat and drink. Also, remind students that we use tap water to cook things like pasta, rice, and vegetables.

### Telling It Your Way

Answers will vary.

### Think about this…

Answers will vary.

### Deciding What Is Important

1-3   Answers will vary.

**24**

*pros and cons*   Answers will vary.

*answer the question*   Answers will vary. Suggest that when students answer yes or no to the issues they have selected, they include some facts and opinions from page 29, and some pros and cons from page 30 that support their own opinions, as well as supporting details they found in the story.

### What's your point of view?

Answers will vary. Students should now assimilate all facts and opinions from the story, activities, and class discussions to form their own points of view on the issue. As they present their points of view, they should be able to give supporting details as to why they feel the way they do. Discuss the different points of view with the class. Ask students if they changed their minds from what they first thought about the issue. What made them change their minds? Do they now see that there is always more than one point of view on an issue?

## ISSUE 3      It's a Crime!

*Summary:*   The story discusses whether or not company executives should be held responsible for the environmental crimes of their companies. Many people feel that executives should be held responsible because, after all, someone needs to take responsibility. But lots of executives feel this is unfair because many times these crimes are accidents and executives have taken every precaution to avoid them. Unfortunately, they still happen. In addition to the question, "Should executives be held responsible?", there is also the predicament of *how* they should be held responsible. Should they be incarcerated? Should they be required to attend awareness meetings? In conclusion, everyone needs to become more educated about responsibility and environmental crimes in the workplace.

*Background Information:*   This story explores legal implications associated with crimes against the environment. Students discover that people can be held responsible for damages against the natural world caused by others in their company. Often, stiff fines are assessed against both the company and the people in charge. The money is then used to correct the damages. Topics for further discussion:

- To what extent should a corporation be held liable for an employee's crime against the environment?
- What kind of laws can help protect the environment?

### ENRICHMENT ACTIVITY

Hold a mock trial in the classroom. The trial will determine whether Pat Profit should be held accountable for pollution of a local lake. Her company, Hair Products for You, makes hair dyes. A recent malfunction at her plant caused large amounts of hair dye to discharge into the lake. This polluted the lake and killed many species of plants and animals in the water environment. Pat's attorney, Dave Defender, has evidence to prove that the discharge was caused when a plant worker mistakenly turned a switch. Assign volunteers to take the roles of Pat Profit and Dave Defender. A third student acts as the town attorney, Rita Right, who represents the local community. Conclude the trial with a class vote to determine the verdict.

## ESL/LEP ACTIVITY

Pair each ESL/LEP student with a native English speaker. Have them review each word listed in the *Words to Know* and its definition. Then, ask the pairs to use each term in a sentence. Have the pairs swap sentences. Ask the native English speaker to read each sentence aloud, omitting the term from the *Words to Know*. His or her partner must then name the word needed to complete the sentence.

## *Answer Key*

*Checking Your Understanding*
1. c, 2. b, 3. b, 4. a

*Choosing an Issue*
Answers will vary.

*Getting the Facts*
*Look*
1. They think that executives should not be liable for their company's crime.
2. 5%
3. Most people (the majority) think executives should be held liable for their company's crime.

*Listen to others*
Answers will vary. Answers should include information on recycling, any environment-related class trips, or assemblies that students have encountered recently.

*Remember the Facts*
1. F/Some people think that if a company pollutes, the executives should be held liable.
2. T
3. F/When ten barrels of oil spilled to the earth, the owner of the company was found guilty of the crime.
4. F/Judges are sending people to meetings to learn about how to protect the land and water, and how to stop pollution.
5. F/Half of the executives feel they are responsible for environmental crimes.
6. T

*Ask Questions*
*what I want to know* Answers will vary. Possible answer: How does the river become polluted?

*how I will find more information* Answers will vary. Possible answer: contact the Environmental Protection Agency or a local environmental protection agency

*choose own topic*

*topic* oceans with oil spilled in them

*what I want to know* How does the oil affect the plant and animal life?

*what I already know* Most animals look like they are dying

*how I will find out* I will go to my local library or contact a local water agency to find out who to contact.

*Organizing the Information*
*not supporting details*
We all live in an environment.
Hunters like to hunt in the right places.
Students need to know about testing blood.
*putting things in order* 2, 1, 3

*what finally happened* The owner of the company was held liable for the crime even though it was an accident and he was heavily fined.

*word that best describes* 2, 3, 4, 1

*Taking a Closer Look*
1. ~~pollution~~/hunting
2. ~~none~~/half
3. ~~jail~~/meetings
4. ~~freed~~/punished
5. ~~judges~~/people
*choose statement that is a fact/opinion* Answers will vary.

*pros/cons* 1. pro, 2. con, 3. con, 4. pro, 5. pro, 6. con

*write the numbers of pros/cons*
*pros* 1, 4, 5,
*cons* 2, 3, 6

*writing opinions*
*why people should be held liable for polluting the environment* Answers will vary. Possible answers: *(pros)* People should be liable for polluting the environment because someone needs to be responsible for these incidents when they happen. Sometimes the government has to clean up environmental accidents even though they were caused by companies. This costs taxpayers money. When companies dump dangerous chemicals into a river, they are poisoning our drinking water so they should be held responsible. People who destroy the land and water are destroying an important resource so they should be held accountable for this and be aware of what they are doing. Children need to be taught how to protect the land so that they can make informed decisions and help others become aware.

*why people should not be held liable for polluting the environment* Answers will vary. Possible answers: *(cons)* People should not be liable for polluting the environment because sometimes the polluting is a result of an accident, and executives should not be blamed for something that they are not aware of and that they didn't do on purpose. Also, people should still be able to do things that they like to do, even though there is a small chance that that act could harm the environment. For example, hunters feel that they should have the right to hunt anywhere they want.

*why is it a good idea* Answers will vary. Possible answers: *(pros and cons)* It is a good idea for everyone to learn more about the environment because when companies dump dangerous chemicals into a river, they are poisoning our drinking water, so they need to be taught how to protect the land and water. Company executives should not be blamed for accidents they are not aware of, but if they learn more about the environment, then less accidents would probably happen. Accidents have to be cleaned up no matter who caused them, so everyone should learn more about how to prevent accidents. People who are polluting the land are destroying an important resource. Education would help control pollution.

*what can be done* Answers will vary. Possible answers: educating people/joining organizations/pitching in

*cause/effect* 2, 1; 2, 1; 1, 2; 2, 1; 1, 2

*another cause and effect* Answers will vary. Possible answer: *(cause)* Police found tainted vials of blood dumped on the beach by the owner of a blood-testing company. *(effect)* He was charged for this crime.

## Thinking Other Ways
1. b, 2. c, 3. a, 4. b, 5. c

*if Tina threw oil down the drain* Answers will vary. Possible answer: The oil would get into our waters.

*if Dave used ink with oil* Answers will vary. Possible answer: He would have to recycle it.

*if Rita didn't care about recycling* Answers will vary. Possible answer: She would not recycle the paper and a lot of trees would have been wasted for just one use.

*if Juan talked to the worker* Answers will vary. Possible answer: The worker would understand why it is so important to recycle and become more aware of how to help clean up the environment.

*if Kim put a sign up* Answers will vary. Possible answer: She wouldn't have to pick up as many soda cans and maybe their school could get money for recycling the cans.

## Talk about…
Answers will vary. After students share their stories relate them back to the story and tell them that some company executives might feel the same way when they are blamed for accidents that they feel are not their fault.

## Telling It Your Way
Answers will vary. Students should go back to the story or review activities if they need to refresh their memories.

Students should have enough information to support their answer with details.

## Think about this…
Answers will vary. Learning to protect the environment can help anyone in the workplace use and recycle products effectively.

## Deciding What Is Important
1-3 Answers will vary.

*pros/cons* Answers will vary.

*answer the question* Answers will vary. Suggest that when students answer yes or no to the issues they have selected, they include some supporting details from page 46, some facts and opinions from page 48, and some pros and cons from page 49, that support their own opinions, as well as supporting details they found in the story.

## What's your point of view?
Answers will vary. Students should now assimilate all facts and opinions from the story, activities, and class discussions to form their own points of view on the issue. As they present their points of view, they should be able to give supporting details as to why they feel the way they do. Discuss the different points of view with the class. Ask students if they changed their minds from what they first thought about the issue. What made them change their minds? Do they now see that there is always more than one point of view on an issue?



# WHAT'S YOUR POINT OF VIEW ON CAREERS?

## ISSUE 1    Go For It!

*Summary:* This story talks about obstacles and how important it is to overcome them. Some famous people who overcame obstacles, like Tom Cruise, Cher, Jim Abbot, and Tyrone "Mugsy" Bogues, are mentioned. The story discusses the fact that the way we handle obstacles determines whether we will be successful. Some of the suggestions are to keep positive, be patient, think about consequences, don't blame others, take control of the problem, then solve the problem. If the goal is really too difficult it should be modified. Whatever our goals, we will all face barriers and obstacles, but we need to overcome them to succeed.

*Background Information:* In this story, students discover that many famous stars and professional athletes had to overcome obstacles in order to achieve their goals. For example, Cher and Tom Cruise both had to deal with dyslexia on their road to success. Other people had to overcome physical handicaps, racial discrimination issues, and even poverty. Topics for further class discussion on this issue include:

- Who do you know that has overcome great obstacles in order to achieve his or her goals? How did they achieve their goals?
- What can be learned by reading about the struggles of people such as Jackie Robinson and Jim Abbott?

## ENRICHMENT ACTIVITY

Divide the class into small groups of three or four students. Challenge each group to conduct research to identify a "Local Hero" who overcame great obstacles in order to achieve his or her goal. (Be sure students understand that the "great obstacle" does not have to be some type of physical disability. (An example of a Local Hero might be a senior citizen who receives a college diploma.) The research might involve interviewing community members, reading local newspapers, or even contacting the Chamber of Commerce. Have each group present their findings to the class. You may even wish to invite some of the "Local Heroes" to speak to the class!

## ESL/LEP ACTIVITY

Discuss the meaning of the term discrimination. Develop the idea that discrimination is treating someone differently from others. Tell students that there are many different kinds of discrimination. Racial discrimination is treating someone differently because of his or her race. Gender discrimination is treating someone differently because of his or her sex. Age discrimination is treating someone differently because of his or her age. Encourage volunteers to describe situations in which they have observed discrimination. Have the listeners classify the act in one of the categories discussed.

## *Answer Key*

*Checking Your Understanding*
1. c, 2. a, 3. b, 4. c

*Choosing an Issue*
Answers will vary.

*Getting the Facts*
*Look*
1. help
2. not help
3. help
4. not help

*Listen to others*
Answers will vary. Possible answers:
1. extra studying helps in mastering the material so the student will get better grades
2. won't help student master English, but student will not fail class
3. may help student master material and will let teacher know that student
4. will fail class, but student will not be upset anymore

*Remember the Facts*
1. F/Jackie Robinson had to overcome racial discrimination in order to reach his goals.
2. F/Jim Abbott was born without a right hand.
3. T
4. F/Blaming others will not help you solve your problems.
5. T
6. F/When you quit, you keep yourself from reaching your goals.

*Ask Questions*
Tom Cruise
*goal*   actor
*obstacle*  dyslexia
*I would like to ask*   Answers will vary.
Cher
*goal*   singer/actress
*obstacle*   dyslexia
*I would like to ask*   Answers will vary.
Jackie Robinson
*goal*   play major league baseball
*obstacle*  racial discrimination
*I would like to ask*   Answers will vary.
Jim Abbott
*goal*   be a major league pitcher
*obstacle*   born without a right hand
*I would like to ask*   Answers will vary.

Mugsy Bogues
*goal*   play professional basketball
*obstacle*   he's a foot shorter than most basketball players
*I would like to ask*   Answers will vary.

*think about yourself*   Answers will vary.

*Organizing the Information*
*putting things in order*
3, 2, 1, scrambled eggs or an omelette
3, 2, 1, a telephone call is placed
2, 1, 3, a letter is mailed
*another process*
1. unfold the microwave popcorn package
2. place the package in the microwave
3. put the popped popcorn in a bowl
*put the steps in the correct order*   6, 5, 3, 2, 4, 1

*Taking a Closer Look*

*fact/opinion*   1. fact, 2. opinion, 3. opinion, 4. fact, 5. fact, 6. opinion

*finish each statement*
1. ...dyslexia.
2. ...play major league baseball and be elected to the Baseball Hall of Fame.
3. ...without a right hand.
4. ...about a foot shorter than most professional basketball players
5. ...you keep yourself from reaching your goals.

*pros/cons*   1. con, 2. pro, 3. pro, 4. con, 5. pro, 6. pro, 7. con, 8. pro

*choose best pro and one con*   Answers will vary.

*think about something you didn't finish*   Answers will vary. Students may mention one of the reasons mentioned in the story. Ask if they have a different perspective on that particular goal after reading the story.

*think about something at which you succeeded*   Answers will vary. Ask students if they feel the way the people mentioned in the story probably felt after they succeeded.

*cause/effect*   2, 1; 1, 2; 2, 1; 1, 2

## Thinking Other Ways
Answers will vary. Possible answers:

1. I would never know if I would have succeeded
2. he or she would probably have a hard time ever becoming successful
3. I would never have to worry about not succeeding or overcoming obstacles
4. He might have done something else with his talents/someone else would have done it
5. Because he believed in himself and worked hard, he probably would have succeeded in basketball if he had some talent
6. Answers will vary. Encourage students to use their imagination to think about a situation in a different way.

*three things you can do easily*   Answers will vary.

*choose one*   Answers will vary.

*three things you find difficult*   Answers will vary.

*most difficult*   Answers will vary.

*did you try*   Answers will vary.

*what you can do to succeed*   Answers will vary. Possible answers would be steps taken from the story: have a positive attitude, believe in themselves, think about the consequences, don't feel sorry for yourself, don't blame others, take control of the problem, think about what might be keeping you from reaching the goal, think about the things that can be done to solve the problem, find more information, change your goal because it is too difficult, don't give up, and be patient.

*Talk about...*
Answers will vary. Students may mention some of the same things listed above.

*Telling It Your Way*
Answers will vary. Students may mention some of the same things listed above.

*Think about this...*
Answers will vary.

*Deciding What Is Important*
1-3   Answers will vary.

*pros/cons*   Answers will vary.

*answer the question*   Answers will vary. Suggest that when students answer yes or no to the issues they have selected, they include some facts and opinions from page 11, and some pros and cons from page 12 that support their own opinions, as well as supporting details they found in the story.

*What's your point of view?*
Answers will vary. Students should now assimilate all facts and opinions from the story, activities, and class discussions to form their own points of view on the issue. As they present their points of view, they should be able to give supporting details as to why they feel the way they do. Discuss the different points of view with the class. Ask students if they changed their minds from what they first thought about the issue. What made them change their minds? Do they now see that there is always more than one point of view on an issue?

## ISSUE 2    Looking Ahead

*Summary:* The story focuses on technology and the way it affects our everyday lives and the jobs of the future. It makes the point that new inventions not only create new jobs, but that they take away jobs as well. For example, tiny robots may someday perform surgery. This would eliminate the jobs of many surgeons. Even though many of these inventions will make our lives easier, they still have their faults. A robot performing surgery could not make a life saving decision if something did not proceed as usual during the procedure. New inventions can also cost a lot of money and require a lot of education for people to be able to use them. Will these inventions make our future lives easier or more difficult? Will they create as many new jobs as they take away?

*Background Information:*   While new inventions improve the quality of life, they may also alter the need for certain kinds of jobs. For example, a computer programmer has a promising career in today's world. Twenty-five years ago, when the computer was not invented, this career did not exist! Develop the connection between technology and careers through the following discussion questions:

- ATM (Automated Teller Machines) have become quite commonplace. What effect might this technology have on banking careers?

- What careers could be eliminated by the invention of the driverless vehicle? Are there any new careers that could be generated by this invention? Explain.

## ENRICHMENT ACTIVITY

Tell students that inventions often bring about a need for new rules or laws. For example, the invention of the automobile created a need for traffic safety laws. It also necessitated street signs, traffic lights, and car insurance! Have the students think about the driverless vehicle described in the article. Ask them to generate a list of issues that would need to be addressed if the driverless vehicle became popular.

## ESL/LEP ACTIVITY

Direct students' attention to the word *program* listed in the *Words to Know* section. Have them read the definition aloud. Then, write the following on the board: You can *program* a computer watch to store information. Point out to students that the word *program* in this sentence is used as it was defined in the *Words to Know* section of this issue. Then, write: An usher handed Mel a *program* for the play. Ask students to give the meaning of the word *program* in this sentence. (*A listing of the events that make up a show*) Develop the idea that *program* is a word with multiple meanings. Clues in the sentence show which meaning of the word is being used. Reinforce this idea by writing this sentence on the board: John and Carol argued over which *program* they should watch. Ask students to give the meaning of the word as it is used in this sentence. (*A show*) Challenge the class to provide other examples of words with multiple meanings.

## *Answer Key*

*Checking Your Understanding*
1. b,  2. c,  3. a,  4. c

*Choosing an Issue*
Answers will vary.

*Getting the Facts*
*Look*
Answers will vary. Possible answers:
1. two boys talking to each other using a phone on their wrists
2. One boy is in a place where it is snowing.
3. One boy is in a place where it is warm and sunny.

*Listen to others*
Answers will vary. Any ideas for new inventions should be accepted.

*ideas for new inventions* Possible answers:
1. a TV that lets you change the channels with your voice
2. a car that doesn't need any gas or power to drive
3. a refrigerator with a computer that lets you punch in the food you want so it can serve it to you

*Remember the Facts*
1. Scientists have created a model for a phone watch.
2. In the future you may be able to store information in your watch.
3. Robots may be used to treat wounds inside the body.
4. Treating illness by injecting a small robot into a patient will decrease the number of operations performed.
5. Scientists have created a truck that can move 55 miles per hour without a driver.

*Ask Questions*
*chart* Answers will vary. Possible answers include:
What will it look like?
How reliable is the robot?
How will the beams be able to tell if what they see is a bump or something else?

*write your own* Answers will vary. Possible answer:

New things often cost more money, and learning to use them would require more education.

How would everyone be able to use these new inventions?

*Organizing the Information*
*web chart* things found in the home. Answers will vary. Possible answers:

*VCR* record programs, watch taped programs again and again, rent movies

*Microwave Oven* fast dinners, reheating is fast and easy, kids can cook

*web chart* new inventions. Answers will vary. Possible answers:

*Phone Watch* can call friends anytime, no wires, good in case of an emergency

*Driverless Car* can read while driving, won't have to depend on others for a ride, won't get tired of driving

*good points about the invention of a car*

easier to get from one place to another

much faster than old ways of transportation

can accommodate a lot of people

*bad points about the invention of a car*

car accidents

pollution

gas costs a lot of money, need car insurance which costs
   money

*good points about the invention of the phone watch*

easier to call from place to place

good in case of an emergency

can call someone from wherever you are

*bad points about the invention of the phone watch*

people could call you too much

calls would probably cost a lot of money to make

sometimes people you call may not get a good connection

*reasons why future jobs will be affected in a good way*   A, C, E

*reasons why future jobs will be affected in a bad way*   B, D, F

*choose most important reason*   Answers will vary.

*why did you choose this reason*   Answers will vary.

### Taking a Closer Look

*fact/opinion*   1. fact, 2. opinion, 3. opinion, 4. opinion,
5. fact, 6. fact, 7. fact, 8. opinion

*finish each statement*

1. …just talk into the speaker.
2. …store information such as phone numbers,
   appointments, and directions!
3. …instruct it to heal a wound.
4. …not hit objects.

*pros/cons*   1. pro, 2. pro, 3. con, 4. con, 5. con, 6. pro, 7.
con, 8. pro

*choose best pro and one con*   Answers will vary.

*how new inventions could affect life and make it better*
Answers will vary.  Possible answer: They could help me
do difficult jobs faster.

*how new inventions could affect life and make it worse*
Answers will vary.  Possible answer: They could be very
expensive and difficult to learn about.

*how new inventions from the story could affect life in a good
way*   Answers will vary.  Possible answer: They could
create lots of new jobs.

*how new inventions from the story could affect life in a bad way*
Answers will vary.  Possible answer: They could take
away the kind of job I hope to have in the future.

*cause/effect*   1, 2;  1, 2;  2, 1;  1, 2;  2, 1

*what would effect be*   Answers will vary.  Possible answers
include: Many truck drivers would be out of jobs/It
would make getting around easier and faster.

*Thinking Other Ways*

Answers will vary.  Possible answers:

1. People would have to work closer to home.
2. Lots of kids would probably be going places by
   themselves.
3. People would be talking on the phone a lot more.
4. A lot of doctors would be out of jobs.
5. A lot of people who used to drive trucks might learn
   how to repair the driverless trucks when they broke.
6. Answers will vary.  Encourage students to use their
   imagination to think of situations in different ways.
7. Answers will vary.  Encourage students to use their
   imagination to think of situations in different ways.
8. People would probably have robots doing work that
   they didn't want to do themselves.

### Talk about…

Answers will vary.  Mention to students that most people
usually have many different jobs in their lives.

### Telling It Your Way

Answers will vary.

### Think about this…

Answers will vary.

### Deciding What Is Important

1-3   Answers will vary.

*pros/cons*   Answers will vary.

*answer the question*  Answers will vary.  Suggest that when
students answer yes or no to the issues they have selected, they include some good and bad points about inventions on page 29, reasons how jobs will be affected on
page 30, some facts and opinions from page 31, and some
pros and cons from page 32 that support their own opinions, as well as supporting details they found in the story.

### What's your point of view?

Answers will vary.  Students should now assimilate all
facts and opinions from the story, activities, and class discussions to form their own points of view on the issue.  As
they present their points of view, they should be able to
give supporting details as to why they feel the way they
do.  Discuss the different points of view with the class.
Ask students if they changed their minds from what they
first thought about the issue.  What made them change
their minds?  Do they now see that there is always more
than one point of view on an issue?

## ISSUE 3    More Jobs or Good Jobs?

*Summary:* The story discusses the state of unemployment in our society and other societies today,
what causes it, and what kinds of options we have
to improve it.  In Europe, wages have been growing,
but few new jobs are being created.  In the United

States, millions of new jobs are being created, but wages are low. So, while many Americans are working, their salaries are low. The story makes the point that technology is what is causing these problems. Machines are taking the place of workers. This allows companies to remain competitive and saves them money, but it hurts employees. Should there be limits on the number of machines companies can use? What else can be done? Education may be the answer. People need to learn new skills as old jobs become obsolete.

**Background Information:** This story explores the affect technology has on the workplace. Students discover that companies must stay competitive by selling quality products at low prices. As technology changes the workplace, companies are sometimes using a single machine, rather than a group of people, to do a job. Since a machine does not require benefits or a salary, it is more cost efficient. To a company executive, cost is the bottom line! Topics for further discussion regarding this issue:

- Why should a company president focus on maintaining jobs as well as making money?
- Would you be willing to pay more for a product that was made by a company that only used people, rather than machines, to create its goods? Explain.

## ENRICHMENT ACTIVITY

Divide the class into small groups. Have each group conduct research to make a list of ten jobs that are predicted to be in great demand in the year 2000. The groups should also discover the training and education requirements needed for each job included on their lists. Have the groups create a poster that displays their results.

## ESL/LEP ACTIVITY

Explain to the students that a *prefix* is a group of letters placed in front of a *root word*. Many prefixes have a specific meaning. For example, the word *unemployed* begins with the prefix *-un*. This prefix means *not*. Therefore, the word *unemployed* means not employed or not working. Develop the idea that knowing the meaning of a prefix can help determine the meaning of an unknown word. Challenge students to use their knowledge of the prefix *-un* to define these words: *unhappy, unprepared, unsatisfied, unaware, unable,* and *uneducated.*

## *Answer Key*

*Checking Your Understanding*
1. b, 2. a, 3. c, 4. b

*Choosing an Issue*
Answers will vary.

*Getting the Facts*
*Look*
1. car repair
2. apply in person
3. restaurant/short order cook
4. computer repair, sales clerk
5. Answers will vary.

*Listen to Others*
Answers will vary. Bring to students attention the kind of education different jobs call for. Make the point to students that for some jobs, education is the most important criterion, while for other jobs experience is more important.

*Remember the Facts*
1. F/Workers in Europe have seen their wages increase.
2. F/Since 1975, two million jobs have been created each year in America.
3. F/Since 1975, a lesser number of Americans worked for higher salaries. *Or*
   Since 1975, a greater number of Americans worked for lower salaries.
4. F/Machines and technology have decreased the number of jobs.
5. F/Training programs are useful in teaching workers new skills.

*Ask Questions*
*job best qualified for* 1. ✔, 2. ✔, 3. X, 4. X, 5. ✔, 6. X, 7. ✔, 8. X, 9. X

*one more question* What do I dislike doing?

*Organizing the Information*
*not supporting details*
Jobs in the United States are better than those in Europe. It is up to the world leaders to make more jobs for people. People in France, Germany, Italy, and England have high wages.

*putting things in order* 2, 1, 3

*write three events that happened to you* Answers will vary.

*put the events in the correct order* 4, 3, 1, 2, 5, 6

*Taking a Closer Look*
*fact/opinion* 1. fact, 2. opinion, 3. fact, 4. fact, 5. opinion, 6. opinion

*finish each statement*
1. …has increased.
2. …machines and new technology.
3. …a group of workers.
4. …find good jobs.
*pros/cons* 1. pro, 2. pro, 3. con, 4. pro, 5. con, 6. pro, 7. con

*write about it…*

*(pros)* If I were the owner of a company, I would think it is a good idea to use more machines because a machine can do the job of a group of workers, and much faster. Therefore, my company could cut costs and save money on salary and benefits because I would need fewer workers.

*(cons)* If I were the owner of a company, I would not think it is a good idea to use more machines because there would be fewer jobs for people in the workplace, so unemployment would rise. Also, machines can break down. They are not as dependable as people.

*cause/effect*   2, 1;  1, 2;  1, 2;  2, 1; 2, 1

*another cause and effect*

*cause*  People must keep up with new technology.

*effect*  New training programs are being set up.

## Thinking Other Ways

Answers will vary. Possible answers:

1. I would try to get training for a different kind of job. I would then be qualified for many positions.
2. I could try to get the training and experience that is required for the job and then I could apply for the job.
3. Machines would not be taking the place of people and unemployment would not be increasing.
4. People would probably be more qualified for their position and would not be replaced by younger people with more current skills.
5. If companies were not making enough money to share with their employees, they might not use so many machines.
6. Answers will vary. Encourage students to use their imaginations, to think about a situation in a different way.

*what you do well*   Answers will vary. Possible answer: Tennis

*how you learned*   Answers will vary. Possible answer: in school

*how you can use this skill*   Answers will vary. Possible answer: I could coach other people and help them learn.

*what other skills you could develop*   Answers will vary. Possible answer: I could develop skills in table tennis or racquetball and/or coach others.

*Talk about…*

Answers will vary.

## Telling It Your Way

Answers will vary. Possible answer: American workers today are facing millions of new jobs available every year, but with lower wages. Also, in order for companies to stay in competition with other companies they need to cut costs and increase productivity. This is causing many companies to replace employees with machines that can do the jobs of many people at once. Many jobs are becoming obsolete because of machines. It is becoming critical that people learn new skills through training programs in order to become qualified for new jobs.

*Think about this…*

Answers will vary. Possible answer:

*cause*  People who want higher paying jobs need more skills so they need to receive more training and education. Usually they have to pay for this training and it takes a lot of time and money.

*effect*  Higher paying jobs pay employees more because they are more qualified for the job and have more skills.

## Deciding What Is Important

1-3   Answers will vary.

*pros/cons*   Answers will vary.

*answer the question*  Answers will vary. Suggest that when students answer yes or no to the issues they have selected, they include some facts and opinions from page 50, and some pros and cons from page 51 that support their own opinions, as well as supporting details they found in the story.

## What's your point of view?

Answers will vary. Students should now assimilate all facts and opinions from the story, activities, and class discussions to form their own points of view on the issue. As they present their points of view, they should be able to give supporting details as to why they feel the way they do. Discuss the different points of view with the class. Ask students if they changed their minds from what they first thought about the issue. What made them change their minds? Do they now see that there is always more than one point of view on an issue?

**GLOBE FEARON EDUCATIONAL PUBLISHER**
A Division of Simon & Schuster
Upper Saddle River, New Jersey